Firearm Safety

BY SAMANTHA S. BELL

childsworld.com

Published by The Child's World®
800-599-READ • www.childsworld.com

Copyright © 2024 by The Child's World®
All rights reserved. No part of this book may be reproduced or utilized in any form or by any means without written permission from the publisher.

Photography Credits
Photographs ©: Maksim Safaniuk/Shutterstock Images, cover, 1; Steve Oehlenschlager/Shutterstock Images, 5; Shutterstock Images, 6 (top), 6 (middle), 6 (bottom), 11, 19; M. Arkhipov/Shutterstock Images, 9; iStockphoto, 13; Vera Larina/Shutterstock Images, 14; Roman Chazov/Shutterstock Images, 15; Pavel Rodimov/Alamy, 17; Rich Legg/iStockphoto, 18; Kenshi Design/Shutterstock Images, 20

ISBN Information
9781503869790 (Reinforced Library Binding)
9781503880993 (Portable Document Format)
9781503882300 (Online Multi-user eBook)
9781503883611 (Electronic Publication)

LCCN 2022951133

Printed in the United States of America

ABOUT THE AUTHOR

Samantha S. Bell has written more than 130 nonfiction books for kids. She lives with her family in the foothills of the Blue Ridge Mountains, where they spend a lot of time enjoying the wild outdoors.

CONTENTS

CHAPTER ONE
Safety Is for Everyone . . . 4

CHAPTER TWO
Safety Basics . . . 10

CHAPTER THREE
Hunting with Guns . . . 16

GLOSSARY . . . 22

FAST FACTS . . . 23

ONE STRIDE FURTHER . . . 23

FIND OUT MORE . . . 24

INDEX . . . 24

CHAPTER ONE

Safety Is for Everyone

Jackson was excited about spending the day with his friend Brice. Brice had moved into Jackson's neighborhood a few months ago. The boys had a lot in common. They both loved hunting and preferred guns instead of bows and arrows. Today, the boys and their dads were going deer hunting.

Once they arrived at their hunting spot, Jackson and Brice unloaded their gear. They slipped on blaze orange hunting vests. The bright color was easy for other hunters to see. Wearing it helped prevent other hunters from accidentally shooting in the group's direction. Then Jackson and Brice packed water bottles, binoculars, and first-aid kits in their backpacks. Their dads carried the bullets for the shotguns in their packs. Finally, Jackson and Brice took out their rifles. Even though the guns were not loaded, the boys made sure to always keep them pointed in a safe direction. This would prevent anyone from getting hurt.

Hunters must handle firearms carefully and communicate with other hunters before shooting. Hunters should only shoot at targets within their safe shooting zone.

PARTS OF A GUN

Modern firearms have several basic parts. The barrel is a tube that the bullet passes through. On rifles and shotguns, the stock supports the barrel.

"Ready?" Jackson's dad asked. "Yeah!" said Jackson and Brice. They helped their dads set up a deer blind. A blind is a small shelter that hides a hunter. The boys and their dads sat inside the blind, waiting for deer to pass by.

While they waited, the boys compared rifles. "That's a nice gun," Jackson whispered to Brice. "I've never seen it before."

"We keep it locked in a gun cabinet at home," said Brice. "I know how to use guns safely. But someone visiting our home might not. We don't want anyone to get hurt."

Jackson nodded. His dad kept their rifles locked away, too. He knew it was important to store guns safely at home. It helped prevent accidents.

Suddenly, Jackson's dad nudged him. A doe, or female deer, was walking near the blind. Jackson looked at Brice, who nodded.

Jackson raised his gun and watched the doe. He also paid attention to what was behind the doe. If he missed the deer, the bullet might hit something else, such as another animal. If the bullet hit something hard, such as a rock or tree trunk, it could **ricochet** and hit a person in their group. Jackson needed to aim carefully in order to hit the deer.

Finally, Jackson put his finger on the trigger of his gun and fired. The deer fell. "Great shot!" Brice said. Jackson smiled. "You'll get the next one," he said.

OTHER TYPES OF GUNS

Many young people have guns that do not use bullets, such as BB guns and air guns. These types of guns shoot pellets or other small **projectiles**. Some use the force of a spring that has been pulled back. Others use pressure from a gas canister to shoot out pellets. But these guns can still fire at the same speed as traditional guns. Because of this, they can hurt someone if used incorrectly. Every year, thousands of people are injured by BB guns and air guns. People who use them should always follow gun safety guidelines.

Like Jackson and Brice's families, many people use firearms for hunting. Firearms include handguns, shotguns, and rifles. Others buy these guns for protection. Some people, such as police officers, may have to use firearms for their jobs.

Anyone who owns a gun is responsible for using and storing it safely. But gun owners are not the only people who should know about firearm safety. People who do not own guns should know about safe gun handling, too. Every year, people are injured and even killed by accidental gunshots. In many of these situations, the shooter is a family member or friend. The shooter might not be following proper gun safety guidelines. Whether at home or in the woods, knowing what to do when there are guns nearby can help people avoid a tragedy.

To prevent accidents, hunters should stay focused and alert while using firearms. They should always be aware of their surroundings.

CHAPTER TWO

SAFETY BASICS

A person who owns a firearm must know how to handle and store it safely. Many firearm accidents in homes happen because a gun was not put away properly. Sometimes parents overlook gun storage guidelines. They may think their children can tell the difference between real guns and toys. Or they may believe firearms are out of kids' reach. But many accidents happen because children can get to the guns. Even if everyone in a home knows how to use a gun, it is important to store guns safely. That way, people visiting the home will be safe, too.

To safely store a firearm, a person should first unload the **ammunition**. Bullets should be placed in a separate container than the gun. The firearm should be locked in a gun case, cabinet, or safe. If a person is visiting a home where there are guns, he should ask the owner how the firearms are stored.

Some hunters purchase special cases for storing firearms. Others lock their firearms in cabinets or safes. These storage options keep a hunter's firearms protected and safely locked away.

REAL GUN OR TOY GUN?

US law includes guidelines for how toy guns should be marked. But real guns sometimes look like toys. Some manufacturers make handguns in bright colors. Gun owners can also buy **vinyl** covers for their weapons, which come in many colors and designs. Some people think this is a dangerous trend. Children may think the guns are toys and accidentally fire them.

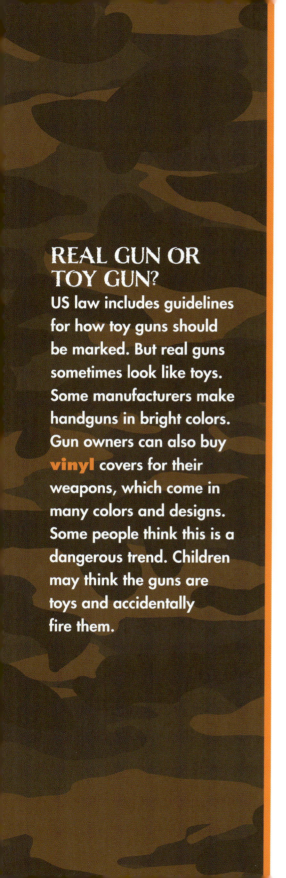

A person should never fire a gun unless she knows how to use it. Both kids and adults can take firearm safety classes. These classes teach people how guns work. People learn how to clean, store, and shoot guns. Some classes also discuss wildlife **conservation**. Hunters learn how to hunt in a way that supports animal populations.

Kids can learn the basics of gun safety through groups such as Boy Scouts or 4-H, which offer shooting sports programs. In these programs, experienced adults teach kids how to use guns safely and aim accurately. Kids can also learn from private instructors and hunter education courses.

Sometimes people may find themselves in situations where guns are not being stored or handled safely. This may happen at someone's home, in a car, or during a hunting trip. For example, a person might leave a gun out on a table or high up on a cabinet.

People can practice their shooting skills at indoor or outdoor shooting ranges. They can practice handling different type of firearms, including handguns and rifles.

Some people compete in shooting sports such as clay or skeet shooting. Shooting is even an Olympic sport.

The gun may be hidden under a bed or in a closet. In a car, a gun might be stored under a seat or in the glove compartment. If a person finds a gun in one of these places, she should leave the area immediately. If a child or teen finds a gun out of place, he should leave it alone and tell an adult right away.

It's important for beginners to learn about protective gear such as safety goggles and ear protection.

CHAPTER THREE

Hunting with Guns

Many kids use guns when they go hunting with their parents or other adults. Some kids even have their own guns. There is no **federal** law about how old a person must be to own a shotgun or rifle. But different states may have different laws.

Other hunting laws depend on individual states. For example, some states require kids to have a hunting license. This is an official permit that gives a person permission to hunt. Most states require kids to take a hunter education course to get a license. In some states, children as young as six years old can use guns when hunting without a license. But that doesn't mean kids should go hunting by themselves. To stay safe, young hunters should always hunt with an experienced adult.

When hunting with firearms, both adults and kids should follow safe hunting practices. They should wear blaze orange or bright pink clothing, such as vests, hats, or jackets. These bright colors make it easier for hunters to see each other while outdoors. This helps prevent accidental shootings.

If hunters do not wear bright orange or pink clothing while hunting, it makes it difficult for other hunters to see them outdoors.

In hunter education courses, kids learn how to handle guns properly and model responsible hunting behaviors.

A hunter should also make sure his firearm works correctly before using it. He should check the **bore** to make sure nothing will get in the bullet's way. Then he should check that all the firearm's parts work. If one part isn't working right, the hunter should never use the gun. Instead, he should ask for help from an experienced hunter.

In many US states, hunters are required to wear blaze orange or bright pink clothing while hunting with firearms. Hunters should always follow their area's rules.

FIREARM SAFETY RULES

1. Treat every gun as if it is loaded.

2. Always keep a firearm pointed in a safe direction.

3. Do not put your finger on the trigger until you are ready to shoot.

4. Know exactly where your target is and be aware of what is around it.

To stay safe, hunters should follow the four basic rules of firearm safety.

If a person is around a hunter who is not handling a gun safely, he should leave the area right away and tell an adult. But sometimes an adult is the one being unsafe. An adult may be drinking alcohol or taking drugs while handling a gun. Alcohol and drugs weaken a person's ability to make good decisions. They can cause a person to react more slowly. Even if the adult is a parent, the situation is not safe. If a child finds herself in this situation, she should leave the area and tell another adult.

Firearm safety is important for everyone to learn. Even if people do not own guns, they still should know how to safely handle them. If more people follow firearm safety rules, there will be fewer gun accidents. Gun safety guidelines can help keep people safe, both at home and on the hunt.

LEAD BULLETS

One of the biggest threats to animals that live in hunting areas is lead poisoning. Many firearm bullets are made of lead, a **toxic** metal. When animals are shot with lead bullets, tiny pieces of the lead go into their bodies. If wounded animals escape and die later, they become food for scavengers. Scavengers are animals that eat dead or decaying things. Scavengers may eat the lead and become sick. Lead bullets may also be dangerous for people who eat hunted animals. They may eat some lead, too. Hunters can use nonlead bullets to keep both animals and people safe.

GLOSSARY

ammunition (am-yuh-NIH-shuhn) Ammunition are the bullets fired from a gun. To safely store a firearm, a hunter should first unload the ammunition.

bore (BOR) The bore is the inside of a firearm's barrel. Before using a firearm, a hunter should make sure the bore of the gun is clear.

conservation (kon-sur-VAY-shuhn) Conservation is the protection of natural resources and wildlife from habitat loss or pollution. By using nontoxic bullets, hunters can support wildlife conservation.

federal (FED-ur-uhl) Federal refers to the national government. Federal law doesn't have an age restriction on rifle or gun ownership.

projectiles (pruh-JEK-tylz) Projectiles are objects shot by a firearm. BB gun pellets are projectiles.

ricochet (RIH-kuh-shay) To ricochet is to rebound or bounce off a hard surface. If a hunter's bullet hits a rock or tree trunk, it could ricochet and hit another hunter.

toxic (TOK-sik) When something is toxic, it is unhealthy or poisonous. Many firearm bullets are made from a toxic metal called lead.

vinyl (VY-nuhl) Vinyl is a tough, shiny plastic that can be used to make or cover things. Some firearms have decorative vinyl covers.

FAST FACTS

- Kids and adults can take firearm safety classes to learn how to properly handle guns. Firearm safety includes using, cleaning, and storing a gun properly.

- When storing firearms, guns and ammunition should be locked away separately. Firearms can be stored in gun cases, cabinets, or safes.

- States have rules about who can use and own firearms. In some states, kids and teens can own hunting rifles or shotguns. They may be required to take hunter education courses to get a hunting license.

- To avoid hurting themselves or others, hunters should always treat firearms as if they are loaded. They should point their guns only at the target and make sure their guns work correctly.

- If a person is around someone who isn't handling a gun safely, he should leave the area as soon as possible and tell an adult.

- Lead bullets can be toxic for people and animals. Hunting with nonlead bullets helps keep both people and wildlife safe.

ONE STRIDE FURTHER

- One important firearm safety rule is to always treat a gun as if it is loaded. Should you still follow this rule if you just unloaded all the bullets yourself? Explain your answer.

- Manufacturers make guns in many bright colors and designs. Do you think this is a good idea? Why or why not?

- Do you think everyone should be required to take firearm safety classes? Why or why not?

FIND OUT MORE

IN THE LIBRARY

Bell, Samantha S. *Deer Hunting*. Parker, CO: The Child's World, 2024.

Dee, Elizabeth. *Hunting Safety, Licensing, and Rules*. Broomall, PA: Mason Crest, 2019.

Hemstock, Annie Wendt. *Hunting with Rifles*. New York, NY: PowerKids Press, 2015.

ON THE WEB

Visit our website for links about firearm safety:

childsworld.com/links

Note to Parents, Caregivers, Teachers, and Librarians: We routinely verify our Web links to make sure they are safe and active sites. So encourage your readers to check them out!

INDEX

accidents, 4, 7, 8, 10, 12, 16, 21
ammunition, 10

blaze orange, 4, 16
blinds, 7
bullets, 4, 7, 8, 10, 18, 21

conservation, 12, 21

gun safety guidelines, 8, 10, 12, 16, 18, 20, 21
gun storage, 7, 8, 10, 12, 15

handguns, 6, 8, 12
hunter education, 12, 16
hunting licenses, 16

lead bullets, 21

rifles, 4, 6, 7–8, 16

scavengers, 21
shooting sports, 12
shotguns, 4, 6, 8, 16

toy guns, 10, 12